Simple Solutions™

Tricks & Games

By
Arden Moore
Illustrations by Buck Jones

Plus Training Tips

BOWTIE PRESS®

IRVINE, CALIFORNIA

Karla Austin, *Business Operations Manager*   Ruth Strother, *Editor-At-Large*
Jen Dorsey, *Associate Editor*   Nick Clemente, *Special Consultant*
Michelle Martinez, *Associate Editor*   Vicky Vaughn, *Book Designer*
Rebekah Bryant, *Editor*

The dogs in this book are referred to as *he* and *she* in alternating chapters.

Library of Congress Cataloging-in-Publication Data

Moore, Arden.
  Tricks & games / by Arden Moore ; illustrations by Buck Jones.
    p. cm. — (Simple solutions)
  ISBN 1-931993-43-2 (soft cover : alk. paper)
  1. Dogs—Training. I. Jones, Buck, ill. II. Title. III. Simple solutions (Irvine, Calif.) IV. Title. V. Series.

  SF431.M822 2004
  636.7'0887—dc22

                              2004003347

BowTie Press®
A Division of BowTie, Inc.
3 Burroughs
Irvine, California 92618

Printed and Bound in Singapore
10 9 8 7 6 5 4 3

Contents

Give Me a "P" for Play!

Dogs didn't invent fun, but they definitely put the "P" in play! The beauty of playing with your canine pal is that you can do it anytime, anywhere. Your dog doesn't require an appointment or that your people contact her people so the two of you can have some good, old-fashioned fun.

By channeling your dog's innate desire to play, you can take the boredom out of basic obedience. Even the best canine pupil can't avoid stifling a yawn after being asked to sit for the umpteenth time in a row. However, if that *sit*

command is part of a more playful game like Doggy Push-ups or Sit, Drop, and Roll, your dog will be begging to comply because you've just made the *sit* command fun.

While we're at it, let's assess those walks you take with your dog. Do you catch yourself dreading these daily out-ings? Maybe it's because you're both in a rut, always tak-ing the same route at the same pace at the same time of day. Even though your dog craves routine, she also detests repetition. Dogs live by the motto: So Many Smells, So Little Time. This attitude may conflict with your "hurry-up-and-potty" mindset. Therefore, your quickie, abbreviated walk shortchanges your dog's desire to cover a lot of ground and leave his "business card" on as many trees and fire hydrants as he can.

This book contains creative but easy-to-learn tricks and games designed to spice up the time you and your dog share together. Consider them boredom busters. Show pleasers. Most of these tricks can be performed indoors or outdoors, rain or shine. For the most part, you won't need any special equipment, either. And here's the best news: you'll discover that your dog will be ready and raring to go at the drop of a leash.

Why Tricks and Games?

Trick training offers many perks for both you and your dog. First of all, you will discover that you'll create a stronger bond with your dog. In his mind, you will be elevated from simply the person who fills his food bowl and gives him safe shelter to the ultimate one worthy of top dog status. If he could spell, you'd earn his R-E-S-P-E-C-T in capital letters. As you continue to introduce more stimulating playtimes, your dog will look to you in anticipation of what new trick you're ready to teach him.

As an added bonus to introducing games and tricks, your dog should commit fewer misdeeds. When you've given him a fun energy outlet, you'll have his brain neurons firing and he'll no longer be bored. Your dog may think, *Why chew on that leather shoe in the closet when I can perform the latest mastered trick before an audience of joggers at the local park?* Success in trick training enables you to say good-bye to Canine the Obnoxious and hello to Canine the Mannered.

Achieving success depends on first establishing a good foundation of learning. When teaching your dog the tricks in this book, keep the following tips in mind:

- **Be in the right mood.** Never try to teach your dog a new trick if you are not in the mood to do so. Dogs are adept at reading stress levels and signs of impatience. So, be upbeat, encouraging, and patient.

- Pick the right time. Many dogs are more willing to learn a new trick when they are hungry and anticipate a delicious payoff in exchange for a good performance or when they are in a "please play with me" mood. Resist trying to teach your dog how to jump through your arms after he's gobbled down a full bowl of kibble or when he's in the middle of his afternoon snooze.

- Select the right place. For any new trick, you need to limit as many outside distractions as possible so that your dog can focus more fully on you. If you choose the living room, turn off the television set and shoo others from the room. If you opt for the backyard, make sure you pick a time when your spouse or partner is not mowing the lawn or planting a flower garden and your children are not outside playing.

- Communicate the correct way. Dogs don't speak in words, but they are savvy interpreters of body postures, voice tones, and hand signals. Therefore, you should work consistently by using specific word cues and hand gestures for each trick. That way, your dog won't become confused and think your signal for *roll over* is the same for *sit up and beg*.

- Praise the correct moves and ignore the mistakes. Were you able to master algebra the first day of math class? Of course not. Step-by-step, you learned by building on your small successes. The same concept applies to your dog. Heap on the praise and treats when your canine trainee performs correctly; on the other hand, resist saying, "no, that's not it" when he fumbles. This is what psychologists refer to as operant conditioning. Dogs learn by association and are apt to repeat an action when it is reinforced with treats and praise.

- **Choose tricks that are appropriate for your dog's abilities.** Not every dog will be able to learn every trick. Like people, dogs display a variety of attitudes, aptitudes, and levels of athleticism. So, be realistic about what you want your dog to learn. A short-legged, long-backed dachshund may struggle to take a bow but shine when you ask him to leap up and give you a high 10 with his front paws.

- **End on the correct note.** Always finish with success. If your dog performs a new trick a few times, don't become a drill sergeant. Stop the lesson and move on to something else so your dog can end the session with a sense of accomplishment.

Walk This Way

A daily walk provides the perfect opportunity to introduce new tricks to your dog. However, before you begin with the tricks, you first must increase your own curb appeal so that your dog pays attention to you rather than to that squirrel scampering up the oak tree, that stray soccer ball kicked in your path, or that beckoning smell of a deposit left on your route by the beagle who lives up the street.

How do you do this? It's easy: before you head out the door, bring a bag of treats cut into itty-bitty bite-and-swallow pieces. Then, make sure your dog knows the *watch me* command so she will look your way when you need her to. Take your index finger and move it up to the side of your eye as you get your dog's attention. When she makes eye contact say, "watch me" and reward her with a small treat. Do this until she associates your hand movement with the verbal command to look at you.

Once you have mastered the *watch me* command, keep your dog's interest by altering the route and the time of your walk; most importantly, vary the pace. Also, be willing to act foolish in front of your dog by using silly voices and exaggerated gestures. You're guaranteed to get your dog's attention and even some friendly chuckles from passersby.

Unleash creativity on your walks with four boredom-busting tricks and games—the Molasses Walk, the Jackrabbit Sprint, Park It Here, and Curbside Attraction. The Molasses Walk begins with your dog heeling nicely at your side; the leash is slack. Then, get your dog to look at you. Take giant strides forward in slow motion as you say "s-l-o-w" in a drawn-out way. The idea is for your dog to mimic your slow stride. When she does, give her a treat and praise her. Say, "good, slow!" Do the Molasses Walk for a few seconds and then resume your normal pace.

Once you've mastered the Molasses Walk, you're ready to pump up the pace with the Jackrabbit Sprint. With your dog looking at you and matching your stride, use an excited, hurried voice and call out, "fast, fast, fast, fast!" as you start power walking. When your dog complies and scurries her four feet swiftly forward, hand her a treat and give her some praise. Say, "good, fast!" Do the Jackrabbit Sprint for a few seconds before returning to your normal pace. Look closely—you may even catch a grin on your dog's face!

Who says dogs must spend their entire walk time on the ground? The trick called Park It Here breaks up the monot-

ony of walking on one surface. Depending on the size of your dog and her physical condition, pick a park bench or sturdy low surface onto which she can easily jump. Take your hand, tap it on the bench, and then use an upsweep motion as you say, "jump up!" to your dog. (She may need your assistance the first few times before she gets the hang of it.) Then, ask her to sit and count to five before releasing her to jump off the bench. Continue your walk and repeat this *jump up* command when you reach the next bench or low surface.

The Curbside Attraction trick can pass the time until the traffic light turns green, allowing you and your dog to cross the street. As a precaution, however, practice this trick on a quiet neighborhood street and never at a major urban intersection. You don't want to put you or your dog in danger.

Stand on the street (very close to the curb, but don't risk getting hit by a car) and face your dog; she should be in the sit position on the curb. Using a food treat, slowly lure her forward. Say, "curb touch" as soon as her front legs touch

the street and her hind legs remain on the curb. At the same time, use a *stop* hand signal like a traffic cop in front of her face so she doesn't continue moving forward. Give her a treat and some praise. She looks goofy with two paws on the street and two on the curb, but this is a fun way to reinforce the *stay* command, especially at long traffic lights.

Congratulations! By mastering these four tricks, you've definitely jazzed up your daily walks. And, you will discover that your dog will likely pay more attention to you and do less yanking on the leash because she'll be looking forward to your next command.

Quick Tricks

The following tricks are designed for your dog to learn quickly and they can be performed anytime, anyplace. They can win your dog the right to enter coffee shops and bookstores and to sit under your table at outdoor cafés. As canine icebreakers they are ideal to use when you introduce your dog to friends, when you need to distract your dog from chewing or digging or other misdeeds, or when you are out and about among others. Amaze your friends and strangers with these simple but effective tricks. In Gimme a Wave, start with your dog in a sit position and kneel or stand in front of him. Place a small food treat (one that he can smell) in your right hand. Let your dog sniff it but not eat it. Touch your right hand (with the treat) to his right paw. Keep a closed fist. At first, when your dog lifts his right paw, give him a treat. Once he lifts his paw consistently, guide your closed fist across your dog's chest to his left side so that he not only lifts his right paw but also moves it side to side. Your dog will move his paw from the right to the left and back again in a waving motion. Say, "gimme a wave" when he completes this motion. Also, don't forget to give him praise and the treat.

If your dog loves to sit up and beg, he'll love the Canine

Paw Me 10 trick, the canine version of Give Me a High 10.

Face your dog. When he starts to sit with his paws up, clap

your hands together and then, with open palms facing your dog, guide your hands up so that they touch your dog's front paws. Upon contact, say, "paw me 10," and then offer praise and a treat. Only give your dog a treat when he makes an effort to touch his paws to your open palms.

Doggy Push-ups combine the basic sit and down motions and take the boredom out of these basic commands. With your dog facing you in a standing position, lure him into a sit position by holding a food treat directly up over his head. Gravity will guide his rump to the ground. Then take the treat and guide his nose straight down to the floor. Scoot your hand across the floor toward you in an L movement. Now, speed up the pace so it is one fluid movement. Take the treat, hold it by your

dog's nose and quickly say, "sit, down" as you then guide the treat in an L motion. Bring your dog quickly back into the sit position and repeat *sit, down* commands until your dog appears to be doing a canine push-up.

Your dog can work his abs with the Stop, Drop, and Belly Up fitness trick. When he is on a walk—or pacing in the house—quickly say, "stop!" as you hold out your right hand like a traffic cop. With a treat in that hand, say, "drop" as you guide your hand straight down to the ground. Once your dog's belly touches the ground, say, "belly up" and draw a circle in the air—in the direction in which you want your dog to roll over. Lure your dog's head with the treat over his shoulder toward his backbone so that he is on his side. Then, keep luring him until his belly is up. Continue the motion until he flops back into a down position. Once he has mastered each separate step successfully—the stop, the drop, and the belly up—you will be ready to try them in one fluid combination.

The following trick, called Find Your Tail, is sure to draw amusement from your dog and your friends. And, it doesn't matter if your dog has a long, swishy tail, a narrow whip-like one, or none at all. With your dog standing

facing you, place a treat in your right hand. Let him sniff it. Then slowly guide your dog to turn his head and follow the treat as you move your hand in a wide circle. The goal is for your dog to follow the handheld treat in a tight circle. Once he is doing this very slowly, speed up the pace and say, "Find your tail." Let your dog circle a few times and then hand over the treat. Stop after a few spins—you don't want a dizzy dog!

When your dog wants you to play—or tries to entice the family cat into a friendly game of chase—he will automatically raise his back end, lower his chest, and extend his

front paws. In the dog world, this is known as the play bow. You can teach your dog to Take a Bow when you catch him in this gesture by saying, "take a bow" and then praising him and giving him a treat when he holds the bow for a few seconds. Once he associates this gesture with a food payoff, you'll be able to say, "take a bow" whenever he is simply standing or sitting. If you have difficulty teaching this trick, try pushing a treat between the front legs of your standing dog as you say, "take a bow." His front legs should go flat on the ground and his back end will rise in his quest to eat the treat.

Dogs love to show their affection, and nothing quite compares to a canine kiss. The Kissy, Kissy trick is a way to get your dog to kiss you. First, you need a volunteer (be

sure it's someone your dog likes!). Dab a small amount of canned dog food or meat-flavored baby food on the helper's cheek. Ask your volunteer to kneel so that your dog is at eye level. Guide your dog to the person's cheek and say, "kissy, kissy" as the dog approaches and licks the cheek. Both you and the volunteer should heap on the praise. Repeat this with food smears until your dog recognizes the *kissy, kissy* command and can deliver a love-filled canine greeting to all those he greets.

A dog who likes to jump up and raise his front paws can easily learn how to say his prayers. Teach your dog to

Say a Prayer by extending your forearm parallel to the ground and having him rest his front paws on it. Direct his head down by placing a treat in your opposite hand that is positioned under your forearm and below his paws. When his head goes down, say "prayer." Give him a treat and praise. Once your dog has mastered these movements on your forearm, you can try the trick on the edge of the bed.

Tricks That Serve a Purpose

Most dogs love to please; they also like to work. These tricks are designed to hone in on those two conventional canine traits. And you can benefit! With the tricks described in this section, remember to break each one down into a sequence of steps. Also, to maintain her level of confidence, make sure your dog has successfully mastered the first step before introducing the next.

Have you ever snuggled into bed, only to realize you forgot to turn off the kitchen light? Show your dog how to help you save on your utility bill by teaching her to Flip the Switch. First, teach your dog to put her paws on the wall. Pat the wall and say, "up." Now teach her *paw* by pointing at the light switch and pawing it with your hand. Then, position her right under the light switch, point to the switch and say, "paw it." Assist her by gently directing her paw to turn the switch off. Praise each success. Finally, let her try the trick without your guiding hands by tapping the wall and saying, "up, lights out," followed by "paw it, lights out." (For short-legged dogs, begin the trick by placing a chair against the wall, tapping the seat cushion and telling your dog "up." Once she can reach the light switch, begin teaching the rest of the trick).

In the Backyard Ball trick, your dog learns to fetch, drop it, and leave the ball so that she doesn't become a ball hog. The goal is for your dog to recognize that it takes the two of you to play a game of ball. This game also reinforces the *come* command in a fun way.

Always start and end the game so that she knows you are the game leader. With your dog off leash in your fenced backyard or other enclosed area, get her to sit in front of you. Then, toss a tennis ball or other favorite retrievable object over her head. As she turns around to go after the ball, say, "fetch" in a fun, upbeat tone. When she puts her mouth on the ball, say, "come." When she approaches with the object in her mouth, say, "drop it." Do not engage in a game of tug-of-war or try to take the ball out of her mouth. Be patient. Wait for her to drop the ball. When she does, say, "leave it," as you motion with your extended index finger an imaginary line between the dog and the ball. Tell her to stay as you pick up the ball. Throw the ball again. If she goes after the ball, stop the game and wait in silence until she sits. The point of this exercise is to train your dog to wait for your command to fetch the ball. This game teaches your dog manners and makes the game of fetch more appealing to you. When you are done playing, give a cue to signal that fetch time has ended, such as game over. You can do this using a hand-sweeping motion similar to what a baseball umpire uses as a signal to indicate that a base runner is safe at home plate. You cross your hands in front of you and open your arms wide. Pick up the ball, place it out of your dog's reach, and walk away.

Enjoy an ultimate lazy night in front of the TV by teaching your dog to Bring the Remote so you can change

channels without getting out of the comfy position on your sofa. This works especially well on dogs with soft mouths—ones who like to pick up things and can do so without leaving deep teeth marks. Dab a moist treat on the remote control and let your dog sniff it. Move the remote all around in your hand and let her continue to sniff it. Say, "remote" so she learns to associate the word with that object. When your dog gently puts the remote in her mouth, give her praise. Let her get used to the remote in her mouth. Gently take it out of her mouth and give her a treat. Now, put your dog on a leash. As you say, "bring

me the remote," let her pick up the remote and then gently guide her toward you with the remote in her mouth. Say, "give" and wait for her to drop the remote in your lap. Give her a treat and praise. Eventually, your dog will be able to complete this trick off leash.

By playing the Find-It-For-Me game, you can teach your dog to find your keys, her chew toy, or other items. Of course, you know where these objects are; that's not the point of this game. The aim is to bolster your dog's vocabulary and engage her in a new activity. At first, teach the trick with each item separately. Place a chew toy (or a set of keys or a pencil) on the ground in front of your dog. Then say, "bring me the chew toy" (or the keys or the pencil). Each time your dog complies, offer praise and a

treat. Now, you're ready to bring all three objects together. Point to the object you want and then say, "bring me the keys." If your dog seems to prefer the chew toy, make the other objects more attractive by smearing a little food on them.

Do you get a lot of large envelopes that require a strip to be pulled in order for them to be opened? Does your dog race to the door in anticipation each time the doorbell rings? You can make Mail Call a time of fun for your dog so that she looks forward to the delivery people. This trick also keeps her from becoming too territorial. When you get a package that requires a strip to be pulled, start the strip on one side, put it in your dog's mouth and encourage her to pull and yank until the envelope is open. Then thank her by giving her a treat and praise. She'll be pleased that she was able to help you sort through your mail!

Advanced Tricks

Think you have a canine Einstein? Do you have a dog who loves a challenge? Or one who loves to learn? Then, the two of you may be ready to pursue PhD's—pretty hard, doable stunts. Here are some trickier tricks that will wow your friends and keep your dog's brain cells firing.

The Figure Eight trick provides an acceptable outlet for dogs who seem to be forever in your way. (It's a natural for herding breeds.) Start by standing up with your legs shoulder-width apart. Your dog should be sitting, facing you. While holding a treat in your right hand, place it behind the back of your knees. Make sure he can see the treat as it's moving. With the treat in your hand, guide him to go through your legs. Then, move the hand  around your right leg, back through your legs, and around your left leg in a figure-eight movement. Your dog will learn to follow this treat cue. If he hesitates a bit, try the trick while he's on a short leash and guide him until he gets comfortable with the figure-eight movement. Add the vocal cue *figure eight* as he moves in and out of your legs.

Another advanced trick—one that is sure to draw applause—is teaching your dog to scoot across the ground. You can teach him this trick, called Crawling, by putting him in a down position and kneeling at his side. Gently place one hand on the top of his shoulders to keep him down as you lure him with a treat in your other hand. Position the treat a couple inches in front of his nose. Entice him to crawl forward to get the treat as you say, "crawl." Once he crawls a few steps, move in front of

him. Remain kneeling as you get him to crawl toward you.
When he completes the move, give him a treat.

If you have a dog who seemingly has springs in his legs,
you can easily teach him how to Jump Through a Hoop or

(if he is small) through your arms. For this trick, a hula hoop is best because it's lightweight, durable, and inexpensive. Start by holding the hoop in one hand and luring your dog to walk through it with a treat held in your other hand. Once he is used to walking through the hoop, you can raise the hoop off the ground just a little but enough to require your dog to jump through it. Guide your dog through the hoop with a sweeping arm motion. Be sure to provide lots of encouragement. Soon, you'll be ready for him to jump through your arms (formed like a hoop). Give him a treat and praise.

If your dog is vocal, you can teach him Doggy Math by channeling his barks into a constructive trick in which he barks—and stops barking—on cue. To get your dog to bark on command, have a friend hold him on his leash just out of your reach. Motivate him to speak by holding a ball or favorite toy in front of his face and acting goofy and animated. Your dog will likely bark out of frustration because he wants you and the object. When he barks, say, "good speak" and give him the toy. Praise him. Repeat the trick until he learns that he is to bark when he hears the cue *good speak.* Never reward your dog for unsolicited

barking. Now, you can move on to the next phase of the trick. Remove the toy from the scene and replace it with your vocal cue. When he knows to bark for each *good speak*, begin introducing simple math questions, such as, "what's one plus one?" (in which you ask your dog to speak and to speak again) or "what's three minus two?"

Then, raise your index finger to your lips and say, "hush" to get him to stay quiet. You can ask your dog, "what's ten times zero?" and he will "answer" with silence. To keep your dog from becoming overly excited and barking nonstop, do not make eye contact until you are ready for him to respond.

Doggy Tandem

If you have a pair of dogs—or if your dog has a canine chum—you can reinforce basic obedience commands in a fun way by having the dogs perform the tricks simultaneously. When considering tandem tricks, it is important to first make sure that the two dogs are compatible—and not overly competitive. You also need to make sure that both dogs are physically able to master the tricks you request.

When teaching tandem tricks, timing is important. You need to distribute the treats (one in each hand) to each dog at the same time. Also, make sure that the dogs have plenty of elbow room so they don't knock into one another during their performances.

Here are some two-dog commands to try:

- beg
- doggy push-ups (fast series of sit, down, sit, down)
- down
- find your tail
- jump over a low bar
- roll over
- sit

It's Show Time!

Congratulations! You've expanded the repertoire of your dog's tricks. Remember to practice patience with every trick you teach your dog. And, take the time to let your dog ham it up and earn some attention by demonstrating these tricks to friends, neighbors, and passersby. Your dog will thank you for the opportunity to garner the spotlight.

Most of all, know that these tricks only skim the surface of what your dog can do. Tap into your imagination and, above all, have fun!

Arden Moore is an award-winning author who specializes in writing about pets and on human health topics. Moore belongs to the Dog Writers Association of America and the Association of Veterinary Communicators. She has authored numerous books, including *Healthy Dog*, *Dog Training*, and *Happy Dog*. She shares her home with her dog, Chipper, and three dog-like cats, Murphy, Little Guy, and Callie. She can be reached through her Web site: www.byarden.com.

Buck Jones's humorous illustrations have appeared in numerous magazines (including *Dog Fancy* and *Cat Fancy*) and books. He is the illustrator for the best-selling Simple Solutions series books, *Why Do Cockatiels Do That?*, *Why Do Parakeets Do That?*, *Kittens! Why Do They Do What They Do?*, and *Puppies! Why Do They Do What They Do?*.